CHRISTMAS SUNSHINE

Various

[ZHINGOORA BOOKS]

This edition is published by
Zhingoora Books.

The Cover is Designed by Pallav Sethiya.

O the angels know the blessed day,

And strike their harps anew?

Then may the echo of their lay

Float sweetly down to you,

And fill your soul with Christmas song

That your heart shall echo your whole life long.

Havergal.

A bright and happy Christmas to you! Lift up yourselves to the great meaning of the day, and dare to think of your humanity as something so sublimely precious that it is worthy of being made an offering to God, and then go out to the pleasures and duties of your life, having been truly born anew into His Divinity, as He was born into our humanity on Christmas Day.

Phillips Brooks.

Most tangible of all the gods that be,

O Santa Claus—our own since infancy!—

As first we scampered to thee—now, as then,

Take us as children to thy heart again.

Riley.

HEN welcome

snow of

Christmas,

We read thy

prophecy,

We know what

wish lies hidden,

What germs of

life may be

Concealed beneath

thy mantle,

All folded close

away,

Awaiting their fruition,

6

In heaven's eternal day.

M. C. O.

One wish ere yet the long year ends;

Let's close it with a parting rhyme,

A pledge, a hand, to all our friends

As fits the merry Christmas time:

On life's wide scene you, too, have parts,

That Fate ere long shall bid you play;

Good-night: with honest, gentle hearts,

A kindly greeting go alway.

Thackeray.

T was the winter wild,

While the heaven-born child

All meanly wrapt in the rude manger lies:

Nature, in awe to him

Had doff'd her gaudy trim,

With her great Master so to sympathize:

It was no season then for her

To wanton with the sun, her lusty paramour.

Only with speeches fair

She wooes the gentle air

To hide her guilty front with innocent snow:

And on her naked shame,

Pollute with sinful blame,

The saintly veil of maiden white to throw;

Confounded, that her Maker's eyes

Should look so near upon her foul deformities.

But he, her fears to cease,

Sent down the meek-ey'd Peace;

She, crowned with olives green, came softly sliding

Down through the turning sphere

His ready harbinger,

With turtle wing the amorous clouds dividing;

And, waving wide her myrtle wand,

She strikes a universal peace through sea and land.

No war or battle's sound,

Was heard the world around;

The idle spear and shield were high up hung,

The hooked chariot stood,

Unstained with hostile blood;

The trumpet spake not to the armed throng;

And kings sat still with awful eye,

As if they surely knew their sovran Lord was by.

But peaceful was the night,

Wherein the Prince of light

His reign of Peace upon the earth began:

The winds with wonder whist

Smoothly the waters kist,

Whispering new joys to the mild ocean,

Who now hath quite forgot to rave,

While birds of calm sit brooding on the charmed wave.

Milton.

 OME say that ever 'gainst that season comes

Wherein our Saviour's birth is celebrated,

The bird of dawning singeth all night long;

And then, they say, no spirit dare stir abroad,

The nights are wholesome, then no planets strike,

No fairy takes nor witch hath power to charm,

So hallow'd and so gracious is the time.

Shakespeare.

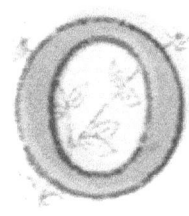 HOLY Child of Bethlehem!

Descend to us, we pray;

Cast out our sin, and enter in,

Be born in us to-day.

We hear the Christmas angels

The great glad tidings tell;

Oh come to us, abide with us,

Our Lord Emmanuel!

Phillips Brooks.

Swell the notes of the Christmas Song!

Sound it forth through the earth abroad!

Blessing and honor, thanks and laud!

Take the joy of the Christmas Song!

Are not the tidings good and true?

Peace to you,

And God's good will that is ever new.

Havergal.

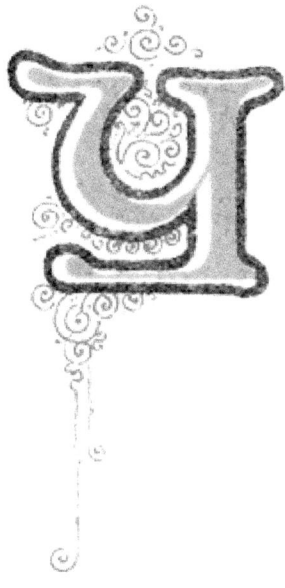

OU little children, in whose eyes

Undimmed the light of heaven glows,

Whose dreams are bright with paradise,

Whose souls are whiter than the snows,

From holy lips and undefiled,

Breathe your soft prayer to Christ, the Child!

And you whose thinning locks are sprent

With unreturning autumn's rime,

Whose heads, like wind-worn trees, are bent

Beneath the savage storms of time—

Pray Christ, the Child, to be your guide

Past the dim shoal, where shadows bide.

O saving hands! O Christ, that hears

A mortal mother's lullabies;

That feels our agony and tears,

Whose bosom trembles with our sighs,

Give us pure hearts and undefiled,

Make us like thee, O Christ, the Child!

Unknown.

ARK! how all the welkin rings,

Glory to the King of kings!

Peace on earth, and mercy mild,

God and sinner reconciled!

Joyful, all ye nations, rise,

Join the triumph of the skies;

Universal nature say,

Christ the Lord is born to-day.

Christ, by highest heaven adored;

Christ, the everlasting Lord;

Late in time behold Him come,

Offspring of a Virgin's womb;

Veil'd in flesh and Godhead see;

Hail, th' Incarnate Deity!

Pleased as man with men t' appear,

Jesus, our Immanuel here!

Hail! the heavenly Prince of Peace!

Hail! the Sun of Righteousness!

Light and life to all He brings,

Risen with healing in His wings.

Mild He lays His glory by,

Born that man no more may die,

Born to raise the sons of earth,

Born to give them second birth.

Charles Wesley.

OD rest ye, merry gentlemen; let

nothing you dismay,

For Jesus Christ, our Saviour, was born

on Christmas-day.

The dawn rose red o'er Bethlehem,

the stars shone through the gray,

When Jesus Christ, our Saviour, was born

on Christmas-day.

God rest ye, little children; let nothing you

affright,

For Jesus Christ, your Saviour, was born this

happy night:

Along the hills of Galilee the white flocks sleeping

lay,

When Christ, the Child of Nazareth, was born on

Christmas-day.

God rest ye, all good Christians; upon this blessed

morn

The Lord of all good Christians was of a woman

born:

Now all your sorrows He doth heal, your sins He

takes away;

For Jesus Christ, our Saviour, was born on

Christmas-day.

Dinah Maria Mulock.

HERE are many things from which I might have derived good, by which I have not profited, I dare say, Christmas among the rest. But I am sure I have always thought of Christmas time, when it has come round—apart from the veneration due to its sacred name and origin, if anything belonging to it can be apart from that—as a good time; a kind, forgiving, charitable, pleasant time; the only time I know of, in the long calendar of the year, when men and women seem by one consent to open their shut-up hearts freely, and to think of people below them as if they really were fellow-passengers to the grave, and not another race of creatures bound on other journeys. And therefore, though it has never put a scrap of gold or silver in my pocket, I believe that it *has* done me good, and *will* do me good; and I say, God bless it!

From "A Christmas Carol."
Charles Dickens.

ARK, the glad sound! the Saviour comes,

The Saviour promised long;

Let every heart prepare a throne,

And every voice a song!

He comes, the prisoners to release

In Satan's bondage held;

The gates of brass before Him burst,

The iron fetters yield.

He comes, the broken heart to bind,

The bleeding soul to cure,

And with the treasure of His grace

T' enrich the humble poor.

Our glad Hosannas, Prince of Peace,

Thy welcome shall proclaim,

And heaven's eternal arches ring

With thy beloved name.

Philip Doddridge.

Christ is come to be my Friend,

Leading, loving to the end;

Christ is come to be my King,

Ordering, ruling everything.

Christ is come! Enough for me,

Lonely though the pathway be.

F. R. Havergal.

 E who have scorn'd each other

Or injured friend or brother,

In this fast fading year;

Ye who, by word or deed,

Hath made a kind heart bleed,

Come gather here.

Let sinn'd against and sinning,

Forget their strife's beginning;

Be links no longer broken,

Be sweet forgiveness spoken,

Under the holly bough.

Ye who have lov'd each other,

Sister and friend and brother,

In this fast fading year:

Mother, and sire, and child,

Young man and maiden mild,

Come gather here;

And let your hearts grow fonder,

As memory shall ponder

Each past unbroken vow.

Old loves and younger wooing,

Are sweet in the renewing,

Under the holly bough.

Ye who have nourished sadness,

Estranged from hope and gladness,

In this fast fading year.

Ye with o'er-burdened mind

Made aliens from your kind,

Come gather here.

ET not the useless sorrow

Pursue you night and morrow,

If e'er you hoped—hope now—

Take heart: uncloud your faces,

And join in our embraces

Under the holly bough.

Charles Mackay, LL. D.

OME all you weary wanderers

Beneath the wintry sky,

This day forget your worldly cares,

And lay your sorrows by:

Awake and sing

The church bells ring,

For this is Christmas morning!

With grateful hearts salute the morn,

And swell the streams of song,

That laden with great joy are borne,

The willing air along;

The tidings thrill

With right good will,

For this is Christmas morning!

We'll twine the fresh green holly wreath,

And make the yule-log glow;

And gather gaily underneath

The winking mistletoe;

All blythe and bright

By the glad fire light,

For this is Christmas morning!

Come, sing the carols old and true,

That mind us of good cheer,

And like a heavenly fall of dew,

Revive the drooping year,

And fill us up

A wassail cup,

For this is Christmas morning!

I N the rush of the merry morning

When the red burns through the gray,

And the wintry world lies waiting

For the glory of the day;

Then we hear a fitful rushing

Just without upon the stair,

See two white phantoms coming,

Catch the gleam of sunny hair.

Are they Christmas fairies stealing

Rows of little socks to fill?

Are they angels floating hither

With their message of good-will?

What sweet spell are these elves weaving,

As like larks they chirp and sing?

Are these palms of peace from heaven

That these lovely spirits bring?

Rosy feet upon the threshold,

Eager faces peeping through,

With the first red ray of sunshine,

Chanting cherubs come in view;

Mistletoe and gleaming holly,

Symbols of a blessed day,

In their chubby hands they carry,

Streaming all along the way.

ELL we know them, never weary

Of their innocent surprise:

Waiting, watching, listening always

With full hearts and tender eyes,

While our little household angels,

White and golden in the sun,

Greet us with the sweet old welcome,—

"Merry Christmas, every one!"

Unknown.

CHRISTMAS is here;

Winds whistle shrill,

Icy and chill,

Little care we;

Little we fear

Weather without,

Sheltered about

The mahogany tree.

Once on the boughs

Birds of rare plume

Sang in its bloom;

Night-birds are we;

Here we carouse,

Singing, like them,

Perched round the stem

Of the jolly old tree.

Here let us sport,

Boys, as we sit;

Laughter and wit

Flashing so free.

Life is but short—

When we are gone,

Let them sing on,

Round the old tree.

 VENINGS we knew,

Happy as this;

Faces we miss,

Pleasant to see.

Kind hearts and true,

Gentle and just,

Peace to your dust

We sing round the tree.

Care, like a dun,

Lurks at the gate:

Let the dog wait;

Happy we'll be!

Drink, every one;

Pile up the coals,

Fill the red bowls,

Round the old tree!

Drain we the cup,—

Friend, art afraid?

Spirits are laid

In the Red Sea.

Mantle it up;

Empty it yet;

Let us forget,

Round the old tree.

Sorrows, begone!

Life and its ills,

Duns and their bills,

Bid me to flee.

Come with the dawn,

Blue-devil sprite,

Leave us to-night,

Round the old tree.

W. M. Thackeray.

 EATH Mistletoe, should chance arise,

You may be happy if you're wise!

Though bored you lie with Pantomime

And Christmas fare and Christmas rhyme—

One fine old custom don't despise.

If you're a man of enterprise

You'll find, I venture to surmise,

'Tis pleasant then at Christmas-time

'Neath Mistletoe!

You see they scarcely can disguise

The sparkle of their pretty eyes;

And no one thinks it is a crime,

When goes the merry Christmas chime,

A rare old rite to exercise

'Neath Mistletoe!

J. Ashby Sterry.

IST and cloud and darkness

Veil the wintry hour,

But the sun dispels them

With his rising power.

Mist and cloud and darkness

Often dim thy day

But a Christmas glory

Shines upon thy way.

May the Lord of Christmas,

Counsellor and Friend,

Light thy desert pathway

Even to the end.

F. R. Havergal.

The End